The Story of
My Suffering

The Story of
My Suffering

*A Collection of Short Stories
of Suffering Children*

Inspired by true events

FURWA J. HUSSAIN

ARCHWAY
PUBLISHING

Archway Publishing books may be ordered
through booksellers or by contacting:

Archway Publishing
1663 Liberty Drive
Bloomington, IN 47403
www.archwaypublishing.com
1 (888) 242-5904

Because of the dynamic nature of the Internet, any web addresses or
links contained in this book may have changed since publication and
may no longer be valid. The views expressed in this work are solely those
of the author and do not necessarily reflect the views of the publisher,
and the publisher hereby disclaims any responsibility for them.

Any people depicted in stock imagery provided by Thinkstock are
models, and such images are being used for illustrative purposes only.
Certain stock imagery © Thinkstock.

ISBN: 978-1-4808-4871-9 (sc)
ISBN: 978-1-4808-4872-6 (e)

Library of Congress Control Number: 2017945930

Print information available on the last page.

Archway Publishing rev. date: 6/29/2017

Special Thanks

Lacey Vargas
Kristen Nazario

Acknowledgements

To my siblings,
If it weren't for you, I wouldn't be
To my Grandmother,
You were love, before I knew love
RIP
To my Father,
Thank you for your unconditional
support and understanding
To my friends,
Thank you for helping me fill the holes in my existence
To all who are suffering,
You can do this

Preface

So much of who we are is based on what we have experienced in life. I don't know if this has been said before, but experience is the most valuable knowledge you will acquire in your lifetime. In the pages that follow, you will read about experiences that left deep wounds, left lasting pain, and holes in our existence, holes that we are still struggling to fill.

This book is not meant to discredit the efforts of our parents. This book was just necessary. It is important for individuals to know how their actions have impact. It is also important to seek medical attention when you start hearing voices. It's important to give up your parental duties when you see yourself spiraling. Get help and communicate with others.

My hope in writing this are: to provide comfort to those who thought they were the only ones with bad experiences; to provide hope that there is indeed light at the end of the tunnel; to convey the message that no matter how tough your life gets, no matter how many suicide attempts you go through, you can eventually deal with what is happening and get through this; and finally, to help start a conversation so no child has to ever suffer in silence. This book speaks from different perspectives. People from different cultures came together and talked about their experiences. There are six different stories that focus on different forms of neglect due to the variety of mental illnesses. One commonality, however, is the fact that we didn't get enough help. We didn't get the right services. We didn't get the right guidance.

My mother suffers from paranoid schizophrenia. I have nothing but sympathy for her now. There was a time when my skin would crawl when I saw her face. I was so angry with her. I didn't understand her illness. I didn't understand how my own mother could've put me through hell and not remember doing any of it. I hated the sight of her, so much so that I developed PTSD when I spent one summer at home. I started getting severe panic attacks because I was living with my culprit and was forced to see her unapologetic face everyday.

So if you read these true stories, if you feel our pain and tear up, don't just clean up those tears and move on, help someone. One in four individuals suffer from a diagnosable mental disorder in a given year. I hope you don't know one, but if you do, make your presence known. As little as a kind word from an outsider would have meant the world to me. Encourage these people to talk about their experiences. Talk about yours if you have any. It's talking that got me comfortable enough to write this. Go get help. Go be help. Go talk.

The Strength In Our Weaknesses

I was sterilizing the milk bottles. In Pakistan, poor families don't have the privilege to buy fancy appliances that sterilize the bottles for you. So I boiled them in a pot. The stove was off so I figured the water had cooled. I pulled the bottle out, which was still full of hot boiling water, and burned my hand. All the hot water spilled on me and my two year old sister, whom I was carrying. I was burned and so was my sister. She started crying, and in an attempt to calm her down, I forgot where I was hurting.

She came running and took the baby from me. She gave the baby to my aunt and started to hit me. She was very mad. I don't know how we started from the kitchen and made our way to the bedroom where I was pinned behind the door. She had somehow gotten her hands on a cricket bat. I think they are worse than baseball bats; they are flatter and bigger, so they cover more surface.

I still remember the heat I felt when that bat made contact with my skin. Hit after hit. I wasn't crying, just pleading for her to stop. The only words I could manage were, "*Meri haddi toth jaye gi!*" I am going to break a bone. I don't know how long this went on; I know by the time she stopped, it was late. She left the room and I crumpled to the floor. I cried myself to sleep that night, right in that corner. What had I done to deserve so much anger and hate? Had I been that terrible of a child? I didn't want to live this miserably.

A few days later, I took several diabetes pills. That was my first attempt. I was only fourteen…

When I was ten

Mental illness is still a huge stigma in many cultures. There are many reasons, but mostly because of the lack of knowledge; these conversations never happen in a suffering household. I was ten years old when it all started. My mother had just lost a child, my second newborn brother. We named him Aun. His umbilical cord was wrapped around his neck at birth. I think that moment, seeing her beautiful child on that cold metal table, lying lifeless, shook her.

I knew that she always had problems. She saw a psychiatrist and took anti-depressants for as long as I remember. She would have bizarre conversations with me from time to time; she was seeing the supernatural, hearing god etc, so the change shouldn't have been a surprise. My ten-year-old self, however, wasn't as wise as my 26-year-old self.

I remember eavesdropping while she told my father that the cat she saw outside had red eyes, that the devil was trying to stray her from the path of righteousness. I remember her showing me this stamp of "fellowship" she had received from the Holy Prophet himself. She claimed to have been the chosen one. I think I believed her because she seemed to know things, things that parental instinct deserved credit for. Imagine growing up in a devout Muslim household, also imagine being part of a society that stigmatizes mental illnesses. Imagine watching your parent have a conversation with themselves and tell you they are hearing from God. Imagine not being able to be alone with your parent because you're so scared of him or her. Imagine them justifying a beating because God himself had ordered it.

Can't imagine, can you? Neither can I, but I don't have to. I lived through it.

She was in such severe depression after my Aun's death. She became very unpleasant to be around. She started being very verbally abusive; every sentence had a curse word. Every sentence told me I was good for nothing. She also started raising her hand at us. I come from a culture where corporal punishment was acceptable, but someone should've seen it. The use of brooms, belts and iron rods that left my skin burning hot and in pain for days was not acceptable. What she did was not corporal punishment. What she did was not acceptable.

I started to mature and take case of the house. I cooked and cleaned. There were times my body would be in pain from a long day of cooking for my family of four, cleaning our two-story house inside and outside, and then finally serving dinner. I distinctly remember this one night, I was lying in bed and I smelled really bad after a long day of household chores. I sniffed around to see the source of the smell. It was my clothes; I hadn't showered in days.

I don't remember a lot from this time but I do remember

a few specific incidents that still shape my adult life. I cooked "*keema aaloo*" one day - it's a Pakistani dish with minced meat, potatoes and lots of spices. It is often served with rice. I made the rice too. I think as a ten year old, that's a big accomplishment. I mean I wasn't tall enough to use the stove, but I put a small stool down and climbed up while cooking. I served the food for her in bed, since she was sick and all. The food didn't come out perfect – the rice was mushy and the curry was watery. She saw the plate, tried to eat it a little, then got very mad. She threw the plate across the room and it hit the wall, shattering. There was very little salt. I don't remember the specifics of what she was saying. I just remember feeling very little. I picked up the pieces of that broken plate with tears running down my face. Even writing this right now sends me back to that moment. I am ten again, with pieces of shattered glass in my hand and that feeling of not being loved in my heart.

My mother's illness consists of hallucinations and paranoia. She hears voices that tell her things others are up to. These voices often tell her to do things too. These voices had something against my father and me in particular since we were the targets the majority of the time. I am assuming these voices convinced my mother that I had a loose character. She in turn, convinced my father of this. Pakistan is known for its honor killings, even in 2016, so you can imagine how big of a deal this was to my father. She also convinced him that I was doing things that would result in a pregnancy. At the age of ten. So they took me out of school and got me a tutor after I had received a significant number of days to "think over my actions."

We lived close to a school, so I would stand on the roof and see kids go in and out of the building. I saw them walking to school in the morning in their clean uniforms, in their little groups of friends. I would hear the period bells ring every now and then. I remember being restless in those first eight hours of every weekday. I wanted to be one of those children, walking to school. Maybe escape my house for a few hours.

Maniya

My permanent molars were growing in, so maybe I was six or seven. I was in a lot of pain. I had my head in her lap. She used to caress my scalp in a way that made everything in this world ok. We were on the couch. She was planning where to spend her night, and I was quietly lying there in pain, just taking the comfort in. "You are a very strong girl," she would whisper from time to time. This moment is still my happy place.

In all the sadness that was my life, my only refuge was Maniya. She was my maternal grandmother. She was a school principal, a petite old lady with short, edgy hair. She used to dominate every inch when she walked into a room - her presence was Zen and matriarchal intimidation all in one. She would put her leg up on the table and smoke a cigarette in a room full of men. Reading this might not be a big deal now, but back in the early 90's in Pakistan, this was a pretty big deal. She was a walking, breathing rebellion against every form of oppression my culture subjects women to. If you know me, now you know where I get it from.

She used to live right next door. My mom broke the adjoining wall down, and we'd cross over and end up in our sanctuary. She would wake up early and cook breakfast for us. The days she and my mother were fighting, we'd go without breakfast or lunch. Now, reading this in America, it sounds very normal, but in Pakistan schools don't provide free breakfast or lunch. So we'd pretty much be hungry until we got home, I cooked, and we ate.

Maniya was the maternal love we didn't receive from our own mother. She would stop our parents from hitting us. She would hug us. She would sit us down and have conversations with us. She treated us like human beings. Naturally, we started spending more and more time with her. My mother didn't like this. She would pick fights with Maniya and then stop us from seeing her. She would tell me that my grandmother was a "*ghandi aurat*," a woman of bad character. "*Shaitan* (devil) picks a wife and daughter each year, Maniya is the wife and you are the daughter," she'd say. She'd build that wall up again from time to time. Keep us away from our sanctuary.

The Big Move

Eventually my father got a promotion. We were going to move to New York. I was 12 when we found out. This was going to be the big opportunity. This would change our lives for the better. We started preparing for the move. In early 2003, we found out that my mom was finally pregnant again. Things were about to be so different - my mom was finally happy, I was about to get another sibling; we were moving to the land of opportunity — what else could I ask for? By this point, I didn't even mind the cleaning and the cooking; everything had become second nature. I was also back in school. This was going to be my time.

As the move came closer, my parents started fighting a lot, worse than I had ever seen them fight before. I think my mother was uncomfortable moving to New York because she'd be away from her family and in the midst of my father's family. She started to pin my dad and me against each other more often now. She would tell me these absurd stories about my dad wanting to kill the baby. She would tell me that she saw my dad walking the house with a knife at night. We were always very scared of our father but this drove us miles apart. Pushing, shoving, fighting, we finally made our way here.

Looking back, I realize that my mother kept us away from positive role models. She hated my dad's older sister and would tell us horror stories about her. She kept us away from all our cousins. She kept us away from our grandmother and even her own sister. In all her sickness, she was still strategizing. I sometimes wonder if she was sick back then too or just a really bad person.

Now that we were in New York, things weren't necessarily better. She was blowing up due to her pregnancy and wasn't able to do much. I don't remember her being physically abusive at this time, so life at home was just simpler. I would cook, clean, watch TV, and just go to school. Oh God, school. I was a teenager without any guidance, an immigrant in the American school system, post 9/11. I didn't know how to dress like a normal teenager. Growing through all those teenage emotions and having no one to talk to, I started becoming quieter. Puberty is hard enough as it is - to not have a mother tell me I am beautiful or to talk boys with was pretty miserable. I think friends would've helped the situation, but I didn't have any. There was zero social development in me because all I ever did was cook and clean. How would I make normal conversations with another teenager? What would I even talk about?

Chotu

My mother was going to have a baby girl. I was there when the sonogram technician told her. She was crying. She came home that night and told my dad that she didn't want to have a girl. Girls are so much harder to raise. She was hysterical. I was lying down next to her. Had I really been that hard to raise? I decided that night my sister was going to get all the love I was capable of giving. She would never hear that she was hard to raise. As a child I always thought my life would've been easier if I had had an older sibling - well I was going to be that older sibling now. I mean, I already was. I keep saying "us" - I have a younger brother. Lets call this one Joe. Joe and I are two years apart. We went through all of these things together. He processed it differently. My mom showered Joe with love. There's a funny thing about love — lack of love or abundance of love — either one can destroy an individual. Love needs to be given in balance. My brother didn't get that balance in his abundance. He was able to go outside the house and get into trouble; I think he got some of his frustrations out that way. I hope some day he's able to tell his own story - boy, has he seen things. But through my perspective, his misery was male privilege and too much love, and mine was female restrictions, lack of love, physical and verbal abuse. For now.

My sister was finally here. Her pet name loosely translated to small person. I think she made me who I am. She showed me how to love unconditionally, even though she was an addition to my responsibilities, I didn't mind. Holding her made things instantly better. Even her cries had comfort. I was able to hold her close, caress her, and ironically give her all the love I was never given. My mother would occasionally try to ruin things by asking me if I have "sexual" feelings towards the baby, but fuck that, I had someone to love, someone who loved me. So I had somewhat of a normal year, I mean normal is relative, but to me this was ok. This was normal. I started high school in 2004, and things in high school were just as miserable as they were in middle school. But whatever - I was a teenager; I had distractions.

Then things fell apart... My Maniya died.

It's downhill now

My mother had a lot of guilt when it came to Maniya mainly because of the way she treated her, so this was just the breaking point. She couldn't see Maniya on her deathbed, she couldn't go meet her one last time, and she couldn't attend the funeral. This was it, our lives were drastically about to change. We were about to lose the remnants of our mother. I didn't cry when I heard the news. I had to be strong; I had to take care of my mother and the baby. I had to make sure the house was clean when people came to visit. In the months that followed Maniya's death, my mother got worse. She became more abusive, less present as a parent, and more withdrawn. Sometimes she would just burst into hysterical screams.

Teenagers sleep a lot. There is scientific research done about on how many hours of sleep our body needs. My mom didn't read these researches so she found a direct correlation between my sleep cycle and my hypothetical drug use. She would sniff my clothes when I'd come home. Ask me why I smell like cigarettes. Wake me up by hitting me if my nap was too long. Ask me if I was having sex or if I was pregnant because I was sleeping too much. She eventually told my father all her suspicions. They decided to once again not allow me an education. I would go to school one day and was made to take off the next two days. In a desperate attempt to appeal to their hearts, I'd wake up early, clean the house, make food for everyone and leave it in the microwave. In hopes that seeing all the chores done, they'd let me go. I'd hover around my father when he'd wake up, wait until he told me if I was going to school that day or not. Sometimes he'd walk out the door without a word on my fate for the day, and my heart would hurt. The lack of education was physical pain for me…

I was still fourteen. Still lacking social and emotional development. But apparently I was ready for marriage. I wanted to become a doctor; for as long as I can remember, that was the one professional dream I had. I told her that.

"What will she do becoming a doctor? She needs to learn how to take care of the house. She will get married soon." According to her, this is what my father would say. We lived in a one-bedroom house. We all slept in the same room, yet there was so much distance between us. My mother was the intermediary between my father and me. She told me he had a suitor for me. He was thirty when I was fourteen. He was a car mechanic. He was my father's friend. I asked my father a few years ago if there was any truth to this. Did he really want me to marry his friend? He told me that he never intended to marry me off that young. He told me he never had that conversation with her. But I cried so much. I lived in constant threat that if I breathed too loudly, my father would marry me to the thirty-year-old or send me to Pakistan. Or at least that's what she told me.

Back to Pakistan

We went back to Pakistan after the end of the school year. We were supposed to stay the summer, but we stayed much longer. We stayed with *Mamo* (Mom's brother) and his very terrible wife. She was only terrible then because she made me do a lot of work around the house. She was a also very rude. We were back to being pretty poor. My mother would carelessly spend the money my dad was sending so from time to time we'd just eat *roti* (bread) and drink *chai* (tea) for dinner. I now understand why my *Mami* (aunt) treated us the way she did.

We were in this really backwards area of the city. We couldn't go outside, or at least I couldn't. We were living in the slums, uprooted from our somewhat less miserable lives here and thrown into this small room with no social contact besides that of my *Mamo*, *Mami*, and *Nana Abo* (grandfather).

I used to stay up all night and watch TV. My grandfather was sick - he had leukemia, so my *Mamo* and I took turns watching him at night. I didn't have school so that made it easier. In the middle of the night, I'd go to him and see if he was still breathing.

We didn't really talk to my dad much; we'd just ask him for money because that's all she made us do. He had a heart procedure while we were away. We didn't know much about it. My father was in the hospital, without us by his side.

On November 18th, 2005, early in the morning, I heard my mother screaming. I woke up and ran to the bathroom. She was standing in the doorway, just screaming away in agony. I kept trying to ask her what was wrong but she wouldn't answer. By this time *Nana Abo, Mamo,* and *Mami* made their way to the bathroom, too. My brother was somewhere in the midst of all the worried adults. My mother kept pushing her *shalwar* (pants) down. I kept trying to push them back up. She was screaming so much that I thought she was hemorrhaging so I got down on my knees and peeked between her legs. I saw a round, dark figure. I thought it was her uterus making its way out so I told her to push. In a sudden and slippery moment, it fell in her *shalwar (pants)*, and then slipped to the ground. My baby sister.

My mom had been pregnant, and no one knew. I gathered the baby in a towel and held her in my arms. I told my mother to keep pushing since the umbilical cord was still inside her - thank you, 9th-grade biology! We cleaned the baby and got a maid to help cut the cord. I didn't know I still had more love to give. This child was about to teach me otherwise.

My mom was sick, so she couldn't take care of the baby. I'd stay up at night and feed her. Here's the thing about babies - they cry a lot and they don't sleep. I remember sometimes being really frustrated because I'd be watching TV, and she'd start crying. I'd have to go feed her and put her to sleep again. My responsibilities were added to; I couldn't sleep at night, and I'd have to be up early in the morning to take care of the girls. Sometimes I would get really mad at her because she wouldn't sleep, and I wouldn't sleep.

Even after all I was doing, my mother was just nasty to me. That snippet you read in the beginning, with the cricket bat - well, that was only one day. I had that every day. Beating after beating, curse word after curse word. *Rundi, Chinaal, Kulta, Badmaash.* Slut, Prostitute, Whore, Pervert. Those were her names of choice for me. I didn't even leave the house - who was I slut-ting with?

I'd just had enough of all the abuse. I started to fight back, ask her to explain all the accusations she made against me. This would only further enrage her. My *Nana Abo* took a lot of pills, so I stole a handful. I swallowed them and cried myself to sleep. I slept for 24 hours and woke up feeling very sick. My body was shaking, but this self-inflicted pain was far less of a misery than what she was inflicting on me.

Finally my father came. He came to take us back. She told him that the baby wasn't his; he wouldn't even hold her. He was taking care of us and we were eating better. He also brought a lot of gifts for us; he bought me my first camera. I think I was starting to like him a little. He stayed for a few weeks and made arrangements for us to come back. He had to stay a few more days because *Nana Abo* died.

That didn't shake my mom as much. I think my mom had lost the ability to feel by then. My dad left, and my mom packed up. She fought with my *Mamo,* and he kicked her out of the house. She wasn't close to my *Khala* (aunt) so we went and stayed with one of her cousins. Then we stayed with another cousin for a few days. And then we stayed with another for a month. She didn't want to leave Pakistan. We didn't really talk to my dad and we were really poor again. Teenagers in America grow up with iPhones and all these other cool gadgets. My own younger sisters have the latest phones. I had nothing. No phones, no laptop, no TV, nothing to read, nothing to write in. When you add my mother's constant beating and cursing to that, in front of people?, I wasn't a very unhappy teenager. I started to cut myself, in the little kitchen where I'd spend a lot of time. I would take a knife, a broken piece of glass, anything sharp and make small cuts on my wrists. When she cursed at me or hit me, I would lie under a blanket and dig my nails into those cuts. That was the only thing that I could control in my helpless state.

We Are Back!!

By some miracle, my dad convinced her to bring us back. We got back to a new one-bedroom apartment on Liberty Ave, Queens. We also got back to daily barbaric fighting between my parents. They would hit and curse each other out. He would slam her into the wall, and she would spit on his face. I would take the babies to the other room and hold them close until it ended. Sometimes the fights got so bad, my dad would kick her out of the house. She would call me, blackmail me with love, and ask me to fight with my dad so he would bring her back home. So much love was missing from my life that I would instantly fall into her traps. Have you seen anyone eat a meal after days of starvation? That was me–approval, love, I would take whatever she was giving. I would go to extreme measures. Taking pills in times of distress had become kind of a go-to. She'd get kicked out, she'd emotionally blackmail me, I would take pills to blackmail my dad, he'd let her in on his own, and I would get screwed over with a variety of pills in my system. I would gulp down salt water and throw up, then sleep for a few hours, waking up sick–all because she showed me a little love.

Of course, all these fights made us hate our father even more. Seeing his tall body slam my mother's evil yet petite frame into walls made us fear him more. She would tell us that he wanted to kill her. Naturally, we were more and more scared of him.

"Your father is a bad man; he has sexual intentions towards you." No amount of therapy can make me forget the effect this sentence had on me. I would serve him dinner late at night when he would come home after two jobs. He would accidently graze my hand sometimes, and my reflexes would act as if I touched something burning. This was my father, and I was sixteen.

Misery Loves Company

Life was pretty tough enough as it was, but why stop there? I woke up with gut-wrenching pain one day. The pain was so bad that I couldn't stop crying. I was throwing up water and bile. I was miserable. I asked my father to take me to the ER. He yelled at me and asked me to drink more water (I get kidney stones from time to time). When the pain persisted, I asked him again. This time he listened to me. As I got ready, I could hear him yelling, "She likes to go to the hospital - who is she getting ready for? Tell her to get her ass out fast, I have to work." He kicked me as I was walking because he was so mad. He dropped me off at Jamaica Hospital with my fourteen-year-old brother.

I was rushed in for surgery. The surgeon signed my parental consent form. I would've died if I didn't go to the hospital. My ovaries were cystic. The right fallopian tube and ovary were twisting and turning black. They would have started to poison my body. They removed everything on the right side and removed a ten-inch-cyst from the left. Having children is what women are prepared for all their lives in my culture. Women are punitized for having dark skin or being overweight; they don't get the good "*rishtas*" (proposals) if they don't look like a Victoria's Secret model. Well, being somewhat barren just ruined my chances. So this was a really big deal.

I remember opening my eyes in the recovery room and seeing my dad next to me. I asked him where the kids were and fell back asleep. I think this surgery was a necessary evil. It brought my father and me a lot closer. He apologized for being mad at me that day. He told me I outsmarted him by pushing him to take me to the hospital. There was pure agony on his face. We bonded as father and daughter for the first time.

I was told to lie about my surgery. Instead of the above mentioned, I supposedly had my appendix removed because people shouldn't know that I might be barren.

They sliced open my lower abdomen, a cut similar to that of a C-section. I had a few stitches, and moving was very hard for the first couple of weeks. I was on complete bed rest. I needed help getting up for the bathroom. One day she got very tired of me just lying in bed. So she forced me out of bed. With my lower abdomen still held together by stitches, she forced me to go do a sink full of dishes. I had lost a lot of blood due to the surgery so I was very woozy. I did the dishes. I had tears running down my face. She was right behind me, cursing. She added a new word to her vocabulary: *Banjh*. That means barren, with a really negative connotation, in my language. She would convince my brother to hit me too. He would slam me into the wall.

He once pushed me so hard, the clock fell on my head, and the glass shattering as it hit the floor. I picked up the glass and threatened to cut myself if they didn't stop hitting me. All with stitches on my belly.

The Height of Parental Neglect

For a brown child, conversations around the birds and the bees aren't common. In fact, there are no conversations. You have to come to the knowledge on your own. My household didn't provide me with social skills, so I think asking for my parents to sit me down and talk about what's appropriate and what's not appropriate would be asking for too much. I do not wish to speak ill of the person, as he is deceased and I do not want to violate anyone's privacy by stating names. However, talking about this assault is crucial. This is one of the heaviest psychological burdens anyone can carry. I think by now you know where I am taking this. It was also the height of negligence by my parents. Whether it was because my mother was sick, whether it was because THAT person was old, whether it was because no one believed me when I spoke about it, it was wrong. I can live with EVERYTHING that happened in my life, I can somehow find a way to heal myself, but I don't think I can ever come to a point where I don't let this incident define me.

It happened over time, so there really isn't a chronological placement for this incident in the rest of the story. This was just a simultaneous misery, happening alongside all my other miseries. My parents had blind faith in a man who according to them was a spiritual guide, somewhat of guru. I spent a lot of time around him because either he'd be over at our place or we would be at his place. At first he seemed like he was helping my parents, teaching them new things. I would stay with his kids, and we played while my parents sat with him behind closed doors.

Eventually, as I grew into a woman, right under his nose, things started to go downhill. I think the phrase "things started to go downhill" can be turned into a drinking game, that's how many times I have used it in telling my story. As a woman, when your body tells you that an approaching touch is inappropriate, it really is. I know when an arm is on my shoulder compared to when it's pressing into my side boob trying to cop a feel. I know when a kiss on the cheek becomes sexual, when my parents leave me alone in a room with a man and he kisses my cheek, holds that kiss for a few minutes, salivates on my cheeks heavily, all while holding my face down with both hands. I know there's an ulterior motive when a man in his late fifties asks a fifteen-year-old girl to sit in his lap. I know when he holds me close in inappropriate lasting embraces, fondles the side of my boob continuously, to a point where I kept my arm really close to my body the whole time in an attempt to block his touch. At this moment, I am twenty six, typing this story, with my arms clenched close to my body and I still feel his old, calloused fingers scratching the back of my arms, trying to get to my boob. I still hear his whispers and kisses in my ear, asking me why I don't call him.

He would constantly call me and ask me
"Maza aya tha?" Did you have fun?

Now I know there was no penetration, no rape, and if this had happened once or twice, I would have forgotten it. But it didn't. For several years, it happened every week, while my parents sat across from me or while they left me alone in a room with him. I was so scared to speak up about it. Even if I disagreed with something he said, in front of my parents, my father would strictly reprimand me; remind me how much this man meant to him.

My father still doesn't know.

No one knows...

A note to the reader

I intentionally left an empty page at the end of every story. After compiling these stories, I needed processing space, as a reader, you will too.

Lily

As I absorbed and processed the information from the 40 Developmental Assets and Davies Risk and Protective Factors I experienced resurrected negative emotions that I believed I had overcome. Despite my reluctance to write this story, I learned from this grueling process that I am not a resilient individual and in order to function on a holistic plateau I must face my demons. I believe the trials and trauma I have experienced in my life made me a strong individual; however, I have functioned for so long from a place of dysfunction, it became my norm. As Davies describes, a resilient personality is developed from secure attachments, responsive parenting and positive work models of relationships and self (Davies 63). In retrospect, I experienced many risk factors in my development, which resulted in a disadvantage in receiving the proper development necessary to function in a psychologically and emotionally healthy state. According to Davies, when there is three or more risk factors that a child is forced to cope with, it results in developmental or psychiatric disorder (Davies 65). Some risk factors on a micro, mezzo and macro level are abuse, single parental care, low-income housing, poor leadership in school environments and poverty. Those are just a few risk factors I can recall as I think back over my early stages of development.

Self Reflection

The moment I was conceived in my mother's womb her plan was to abort me. She was forced to become a mother against her will. "Several studies using the Adult Attachment Interview found that the mother's adult attachment classification during pregnancy predicated the child's attachment classification at 1 year of age in 70% of cases" (Davies, 70). With that said, I cannot recall the early stages of my life, but in reviewing the characteristics of an Insecure Adult I could relate to the description of the Dismissive Adult. A Dismissive Adult is one who cannot recall any attachment experiences and currently has a distant relationship with their parent/s (Davies 26). That would correlate with the insecurely attached child. According to Bowlby, insecure attached children have no memory of their childhood; they could not recall attachment relationships, suggesting defensive processes at work. He labels such memory problems as "defensive exclusion of information." It is motivated by the wish to avoid painful memories and stems from painful and negative attachment experiences (Davies, 27).

My relationship with my mother was very tempestuous,

abusive, neglectful and traumatic. What I do remember is being beaten, with a leather belt that had metal buttons on it, for jumping on the couch; placing my hand over the fire on the stove threatening to burn me because I broke her crystal vase. Choosing men over me, never helping me cope with basic stresses of school or life, not even assisting me with my homework. I remember I despised coming home from school and would hang in the streets as long as I could to avoid going home. There was always an uncertainty when I came home as to whether I would encounter outbursts of anger, rage or avoidance; I never knew what to expect. My grandmother was the only protective factor in my life at that time, and I can recall having secure attachments early on in my life, but they eventually developed into insecure disorganized attachments (Davies 17). I received the love and care from my grandmother when she felt I deserved it. Her love was inconsistent and unstable. When she felt I was behaving inappropriately, her love was conditional and she would shut me out and not talk to me. I struggled with the emotional distress of feeling rejected and not wanted. I believed the abuse and neglect were clear indications my mother hated me. I would often ask my grandmother if I was adopted - did I belong to this family? "The lack of parental support and mediation of stressors leaves children to cope on their own" (Davies 71). I began to seek external stimuli to comfort me. At the age of eleven, I was involved in acts of sexual promiscuity, drugs, alcohol and self-mutilation.

One of the risk factors on the mezzo level was the neighborhood I resided in. I lived in a low-income neighborhood, also known as the projects, where it was easy for me to retrieve drugs and alcohol at a very young age. In an effort to help me, my grandmother took custody of me. She obtained individual counseling at Jacobi medical center for me, which I attended every week. I was diagnosed with ADHD and manic depression, and was placed on psychotropic drugs. I attended counseling sessions every week until the social worker broke confidentiality and disclosed to my grandmother I was having sex. I refused to attend any more sessions because the social worker betrayed my trust. My behavior was destructive and intolerable. In school I was vandalizing and destroying school property, setting off fire alarms; I was very disruptive, causing other students to be distracted from learning, disrespectful to all authority figures, and extremely confrontational. I was mandated to see the school guidance counselor weekly. The guidance counselor expressed that my behavior was the manifestation of being spoiled and manipulative and "you just want to get your way." I needed support from a licensed counselor in the school community, and they neglected their role in helping me; they were blaming me for my behavior. Mental health professionals are expected to help individuals such as myself to develop healthy coping mechanisms for their anger, not blame them for their behavior. "In the developmental effects of maltreatment the absence of a secure base in attachment has in turn been related to less exploratory behavior and less behavior oriented toward developing competence" (Davies 78). Insecure attachment creates mistrust in children and prevents them from engaging and learning from new adults. What I encountered with the guidance counselor was another external asset of support I needed and didn't receive. An internal conflict I recall experiencing is taking defensive actions that were not appropriate for the situation. I was in thought-provoking situations that put me in a fight or flight mode where my defense mechanisms led me into serious conflict. I was accused of assaulting a teacher, and he threatened to press charges, but was told I was emotionally disturbed. The school contacted authorities, and I was admitted into a psychiatric hospital. After nine months of being institutionalized, I was involved in a riot that shut the whole unit down and was kicked out of the hospital. I was eventually expelled from school. I was home-schooled and in the process of transitioning into a Special Ed school. I was continually passed around from home to home because know one was able to tolerate me or help me with my dysfunction.

At the age of thirteen my next placement was an institution called Pleasantville Cottage School. It was a group home I resided in for four dreadfully long years. I lived in a house with fifteen girls who were just as troubled as I was. What I encountered and experienced in this institution was not a system built on helping troubled adolescents; it was additional abuse, rejection, betrayal and abandonment which in fact impacted me in a negative way. In this institution, staff members who are supposed to have the credentials and skills to work with troubled kids are supposed to assist them in meeting short term and long term goals created by a team of specialists. This was a system that was supposed to foster and establish secure attachments between children and health care professionals who became the primary caregivers to build trusting relationships for the benefit of psychological and emotional healing and growth. What I experienced was a broken system that misused its power by provoking children to anger. I recall many times when staff members grabbed me by my legs and arms and locked me in what is called a "quiet room" whenever I misbehaved. This was a room I remember being placed in when I was in the psychiatric hospital. It is a place of isolation similar to solitary confinement. The door locks from the outside, and the room is empty with nothing in it. I was forced to sit on a hard, cold floor, as if I were a prisoner. This room is supposed to be utilized when a child is in danger of hurting someone or themselves. Unfortunately, this system was abused by staff members and used to punish children. They would lock me up in this room because I was disrespectful, and I remember them mocking me from the door and teasing me, aggravating me and causing me to become irate. At times, I was confined to this room for days without a shower and forced to sleep and eat in this room. The only protective factor I believe I experienced during this difficult time in my life was a social worker I was mandated to see every week. Through our sessions I became really attached to her, and she assisted my family and me with many issues. The social worker frequently scheduled family therapy groups. I felt my family and I were making much needed progress. In the counseling sessions there were many breakthroughs; I learned my grandmother's mother had abandoned her and committed suicide, so my grandma understood and could relate to the feelings of abandonment. Just when I reached a point of great anticipation that my life was going in a positive direction and felt progress was being made; my social worker announced she was leaving. I had hope that the progress I was making in the counseling sessions with my family would result in me being discharged from the institution, being home with my grandmother. My expectations of being released soon became another difficult situation I would have to cope with. This situation had such a negative impact on me, I began to digress and exhibit my usual behavior: self-mutilation, fighting, becoming irate, and using drugs, which resulted in me being placed in a drug rehab program. I became extremely depressed, feeling a sense of hopelessness, feeling powerless and alone. At the age of sixteen I attempted suicide, overdosed on psychotropic drugs, and was admitted into a psychiatric institution.

As I self assess I would be remiss if I didn't confess this assignment to be extremely challenging for me. Although Douglas Davies's *Child Development* is based on some research and mostly theories, the context covered unveiled some struggles I still experience. Davies mentions physically abused and neglected children have been found to develop a more self-centered orientation and have less capacity for empathy than normal children (Davies 78). As an adult, I have these conflicting emotions within me when it comes to empathizing with people. I find I lack the compassion and empathy to help individuals through their problems. I feel tense and uncomfortable when someone is expressing certain emotions about their difficulties. My desire is to develop the internal and external assets in the 40 developmental assets. I know to be an effective social worker; I must inhabit the qualities described in the internal assets. As described in the 40 Developmental Assets, an adult role model demonstrates self-control, social skills, engagements in learning and healthy lifestyles. They also provide positive expectations by encouraging and supporting a child in behaving appropriately, undertaking challenging tasks and performing activities to the best of their abilities. The positive reinforcement that would've helped me cultivate external and internal assets was unattainable at a young age. Through external factors, I became conditioned to believe what was said about me. A psychologist, after an evaluation, told me I was incapable of succeeding in college; my IQ wasn't high enough. The guidance counselor told me I was manipulative and spoiled, and I was to blame for my constant conflicts. Child workers abused their power and authority by locking me in a room by means of punishment to taunt and tease, as to say I was inferior to them, and they had all the control. These behaviors provoked anger in me towards all authority figures and gave me a distorted view that they could not be trusted, a feeling I still struggle with. Professionals you place your trust in to care for children are expected to provide positive reinforcement and encouragement. Children may have more difficulty establishing good attachments because they carry negative working models, however secure attachments can be established with responsive care-providers (Davies 80). Reflecting on the experience I had with health care professionals and individuals in positions of authority, it was the last social worker I worked with in the group home, Mrs. Jane that had such a positive impact on me. It was she and my grandmother who provided that external asset of support that I needed. Although she resigned and was never able to assist me in achieving long-term goals with my family and as an individual, she taught me and showed what it means to be a Social Worker. An individual is better equipped and successful at the goal and mission of his or her profession when they've experienced and can relate to the individuals that they desire to help.

References

Davies, D. (2011) *Child Development: A Practitioner's Guide.* Third Edition. New York: The Guilford Press.
Search Institute. (2005). *40 Developmental Assets: for Early Childhood.* Retrieved November 11, 2016, from http://elf2.library.ca.gov/pdf/ChildAssetsList_3-5_SearchInstitute.pdf

Running Away

A loud, piercing scream cut through my dream like a chainsaw. I awoke to the darkness of my room. A faint light emanated from the bottom of the doorway. I felt like I was a slave to this darkness. My only consolation was that faint light.

I heard a low howl. It was the wind coming in through the window. When the wind blew, the curtains flew up with a ghostly movement, and the streetlight crept its way into the room.

Was that deathly scream imagined or was it real? I closed my eyes to try and fall back to sleep and that's when I heard it again. I quickly got up from my bed. It was an instant movement with no hesitation. I was wide-awake now. My heart was pumping blood through my system like gas being pumped into an empty vehicle. I was revving up. I opened the door, and the light momentarily blinded me. Why was the bathroom light on anyway?

I heard a distant sobbing coming from the dining room. I walked over and that's when I saw him. He was covered in an oozy red liquid. No, not really red, it was more like burgundy. It oozed out from his mouth down his neck, spread down his stomach, and dripped to the floor.

Blood? No. It wasn't blood. It had to be something else… but what? What the fuck was happening? Was I dreaming? No. Having a nightmare.

My mother was standing in front of him. A river of tears flowing down her face. Did the scream escape from her mouth? Yes. It had to be from her… Who else? She looked at me, and I could see the fear in her eyes, the sadness in her lips, and the disappointment in her brows. What the fuck happened?

"Que pasó, mami?" What happened?

A whimper escaped from inside her, and nothing more. I felt two bodies behind me. I turned around and saw my brother and grandmother gaping at the sight. That's when he fell on his knees and raised his hands up in the air in supplication.

"Dios Perdóname! Dios Perdóname!"

His eyes looked as if he was seeing God himself. They weren't eyes that were staring at something in this world. They were distant. The eyes were staring at the ceiling, but not at the ceiling. They were focused on something. What was this something? Was he really seeing God?

My mom couldn't take it anymore. She started wailing. I looked at her, grabbed her by the arms, pulled her to me, and hugged her with all my might.

"Mami! Calm down. Jairo, call an ambulance now! Hurry!" Jairo called the ambulance and told me they would be here at any moment.

He was now sitting there on the floor. He was in a catatonic state. He didn't seem to notice all of us surrounding him. When he stared at us, it was as if he wasn't really staring at us, but past us, at something beyond us. I wondered what it could be.

I then remembered the bathroom light. I walked over to the bathroom. When I entered, I saw that half of the shower curtain was dragging on the floor, while the other half was still hanging in its original place. I looked at the bathroom sink and I saw the burgundy, oozy liquid flowing down the drain. There was a bottle in the sink, the bottle that contained the liquid, but that was now empty. I picked it up and read it, It said: "DANGER: POISON." It also had an image. The image of a skull, a scary skull, very ominous, and under the skull, two bones that formed an x.

I tried to swallow my saliva, but I couldn't. So, this is the blood-like substance that was flowing down his body. This was what he ingested, this poison. I touched it. It burned the tip of my finger. It wasn't a slight burn either. It was a heavy burn, painful, and immediate. *Mierda!* If this is how it felt on my finger, I imagined how it felt on his skin and insides.

I heard the wailing of the ambulance out in the street. I ran past everyone and headed downstairs to the front door of my building to open the door.

I escorted the paramedics up to my apartment, and they started asking me questions:

"What happened?"

"He poisoned himself...."

"Why?"

"I don't know."

"When?"

"About ten minutes ago..."

It all seemed so surreal. Was this real or was I just dreaming? No. Having a nightmare. When they got inside the apartment they asked my mother the same questions. They tried to talk to him, but he was still staring beyond everyone. Still in that other world. They opened up an orange colored chair and sat him on it. One of the paramedics asked me for the bottle of poison and I brought it over to him.

"Shit! This is some powerful stuff", he said as they took

him away. My mother went with them. My brother locked himself in his room. My grandmother and I just sat in the kitchen, staring out the window, as they drove him away. We watched the sun rise. The sky going from black, to orange, and finally to blue.

"Mamá, What's wrong with him?"

"*Está loco...*"

"*Loco*? But, why? Why did he do that to himself? I don't understand..."

"Ask your mother when she gets back. She will tell you."

My grandmother and mother knew what was wrong with him. My brother and I seemed to be the only ones that were unaware of what was going on. I stood in front of my brother's door and pressed my ears onto it. I could hear sobbing. He was crying. He didn't want me to see him crying. He was older and had to be strong for both of us. He couldn't let me see him as weak. That's why he was suffering in there, all alone, and I let him.

I didn't go to school. I was in high school, my freshman year. I probably would have ended up cutting school anyway, and it's not like I would've been able to concentrate. I would have just stared out the window, eager to get out and find out. Find out what was wrong with him. *Está loco* -the words resonated in my thoughts, causing echoes that bounced around my head like a game of ping-pong.

Hunger started to creep its way into my stomach now. I was starving. It felt as if I hadn't eaten for days, weeks, months. My grandmother must have read my mind because she was already hard at work cooking us some breakfast.

"I'm going to make you guys a big breakfast to help

take your mind off things. Here Junior help me smash these *plátanos* up. I'm going to make you and your brother the best *mangú* you ever tasted. *Qué quieres?* Fried cheese or salami? How about *un morir soñado*, would you like that?"

"*Sí, mamá*, and fried cheese"

"Go ask your brother what he wants"

"I'll pick for him, *mamá*, I don't think he wants to be bothered"

I took the *plátanos* and started smashing them together, mushing them, harder, faster. I saw the image of him inside the bowl of *plátanos*, kneeling down, supplicating, and I mushed it with even greater force. I felt a tear stroll down my cheeks and fall in the *mangú*. My grandmother put her hands on my shoulder.

"It's ok, *mamá*, can you pass me the butter?"

The smell of the onions and the fried cheese started to envelop the whole apartment. It was a great smell. It began to push away the sullen atmosphere that the night had left. I added the onions and butter to the mix. The *mangú* became soft, and my mouth started to water the more I mushed it. It was like my saliva ducts could sense that food was near. My grandmother had finished frying the cheese and was making the *morir soñando*. It was a heavy breakfast for a heavy night. I knocked on Jairo's door.

"Bro, come out, *la comida* is ready." There was no answer.

"Are you going to come eat or what?" Still no answer. I started banging on his door in rapid succession. That always annoyed him.

"Yo! Are you retarded? I'm sleeping, fuck off!"

"Apparently not if you're talking to me right now. Get up and come eat, it will make you feel better."

"Eat? You really think I'm hungry?"

"Come on man, you have to eat, you can't just stay in there all day. Mama made this food for us, you're going to just diss her like that…"

"She'll understand"

He wasn't going to come out. I just tried because mama had cooked this from her heart, to try and make everything better, even if it was for a slight moment. That slight moment… from when I took the first bite, to the last, made me forget everything, but just for a moment. When the last of the *morir sonando* made its way past my throat and into my belly, that's when that slight moment of amnesia faded, and my memory returned. Was I just dreaming? No. Having a nightmare.

"Junior! Come clean the dishes! I cook you clean!" Mama said. She stuck her tongue out and ruffled my hair. Mama was a strong woman. She never let anything bother her to the point of showing. I wondered what occurred in her life that made her so composed… She did have to live through a dictatorship. I guess that would compose anyone. I turned the faucet on. The water came rushing down and hit the plate, which was at an angle that caused the water to splash on me, and it was hot. It burned. It was a heavy burn.

It was noon and my mother still hadn't called. Why hadn't she called? Is he dead or alive? The phone rang. My grandmother picked it up. She spoke in a whisper. I couldn't hear anything she was saying, and the running water didn't help. I stopped the stream, but all I could still hear were whispers. I heard her hang up the phone.

"*Mamá*! Who was that? Was that *mami*? Did she tell you what's wrong?" I was eager to learn some new information.

"It was your aunt. Don't worry, she said they're fine."

My aunt? How did she know what happened? My mother must've told her, but why didn't she call us first? I was confused. I was getting anxious and the slowness of the day wasn't helping.

It was night when my mother finally came home. Her face was tired and her nose red. The first thing my grandmother did was serve her dinner. I let her eat before bombarding her with questions, questions I'm sure she had answers to. She began to eat slowly. Her mind seemed to be elsewhere, but my grandmother's food started working after a few bites. She closed her eyes and savored the food, chewing very slowly; making sure every taste was tasted. She was eating *la bandera dominicana*, that's what mama called it. It was white rice, beans, and chicken madeade with Dominican seasoning and dressing, aunique taste that was almost as sweet as it was salty, a perfect combination of the two. I had eaten already, but watching *mami* eat made me hungry all over again. The food that was left was for Jairo though. He was still stuck in his sanctuary, or was it a prison? I don't know what he thought it was, but to me that's what it was, his prison. A prison where he had incarcerated himself for a day.

Mami devoured her food. She let out a long sigh of relief and gazed at me with worried yet careful eyes.

"Junior, get your brother"

I stood at his door. I was about to knock when he came out. He shoved me aside with one hand.

"I heard her."

"You don't have to be an asshole about it."

"Toughen up."

"Ha!"

I ignored him. I didn't feel like arguing with him. I just wanted to hear what my mother had to tell us. She sat in the living room with my grandmother when we came in.

"Did you guys eat?" said mami.

"I did, Jairo didn't. He's just been stuck in his room all day."

"Oh, Jairo, go eat."

"I'm not hungry. Just tell us what's going on." She was hesitant to speak. She stared at both of us for a while, then looked away, then put her head down, then looked at us again.

"Your father is sick. This sickness is not physical, but mental. It's a mental illness called schizophrenia. I don't really know how he ended up with the illness, but this is the reason why…it happened."

I had not idea what she was talking about. What did an illness have to do with the fact that he tried to kill himself? A death we almost had to watch with our own eyes.

"I think I've heard of that. He hears voices or something like that?" asked Jairo.

"Yes, and other things. He gets delirious, delusional, paranoid, loses sense of reality."

"How is he?" I asked.

"He was sleeping most of the day, really couldn't speak much. He has really severe burns from the poison he drank."

"How did he get the bottle, *mami*? I know I've never seen you or *mamá* cleaning with that." I said.

"I don't know. He must have bought it. It's some type of drainage cleaner. Who knows how long he had it for." She looked away.

"Wait! Wait a minute. This means this wasn't the first time this happened. Right? When we were younger you told us he got robbed in his old jewelry store… and that the robbers had sliced him up. He was gone away for a few months, and when we saw him again he had scars. Scars on his neck and wrists. He had done it to himself, right…? Right!?" said Jairo.

"Ye— Yes, I'm sorry. I was only trying to protect you."

"And *mamá*, you knew about this" said Jairo.

"Yes *mijo*, but you have to understand you were too young to be told the truth. We had to protect you, both of you."

Jairo was angry. The contorted look on his face showed it. He was yelling, and his face had turned red from the lack of oxygen he was forgetting to breathe in. I was mad too. They had lied to us about something important. They had good reasons, valid reasons, but still. That day they had told us about the "robbery" was the only day I remembered being this angry. I was mad at the robbers for almost killing my father, but in reality he was his own robber. What I had known was a lie, and the truth was even worse than that lie. I see why they never told us…

"There's something else... this illness is generative, it can be passe—"

"No! Fuck that! I'll never be like him" Jairo said.

"Jairo! Don't say that! He's still your father!" *Mami* said.

Jairo walked out of the apartment, slamming the door as hard as he could, causing a mini-earthquake in the apartment. I locked myself in my room.

I didn't know if tragedies were supposed to bring a family together or apart, but things were never the same again. Neither Jairo nor I saw our father for the next two months. I didn't see him because I was scared and wasn't ready, and Jairo, he just didn't want to see him. He was ashamed of him. Ashamed of this family, and I couldn't blame him really. Jairo was too stubborn, and he started getting into a lot of trouble in school after that day. He fought almost every other day, and it seemed like we got a call from the school every week. Your son this, your son that. Mami started growing tired of it, but Jairo didn't care and didn't listen to any advice that she had to give him. He found his own way of coping too, with herbal medicine. I found different ways. I would sink myself into books, immerse myself in their fantasy, instead of living in my reality.

Mamá and I were still close. I couldn't see myself in this house without her. *Mami* had become bitchy, mainly because of all the shit Jairo was pulling. She complained about everything. Nothing was good enough for her now.

"The dishes are dirty; stop reading those damn books and help around the house; control your brother; be a real man and get a job, we need money."

"*CONO*, I'm just fourteen!"

I went to church with my grandmother most Sundays. The aura that I felt when I stepped into the immaculate halls of the church filled me with hope. The high Poman ceilings, the colorful tinted windows with their godly figures, Jesus high on his crucifix, all these things gave me a sense of life, even if only for an hour. After church, my grandmother and I went to eat *pastelitos* in a park and talk about many different things: my mother, Jairo, life in DR, what the passersby were thinking. We would never mention my father, though, or anything that had to do with that night. When we had nothing to talk about; we would just sit on the park bench and watch the people pass by while we ate.

After the two months had passed, he finally came home. I was scared and nervous and didn't know what to expect. When he came in through the apartment door, it was as if a stranger had stepped in. His hair was a mixture of black and gray, the colors fighting over territory, and gray was winning. His eyes cast a shadow on his face, and the remnants of the poison still lingered. He didn't say anything when he came in. He just cast a quick glance at us, nodded, and quickly turned away. I didn't know what to do. *Mami* also came in with him. She walked with her arms around his. They looked as if they were walking down the aisle to get married.

"Come, come, dinner is served. You probably miss my old Dominican cooking, right?" *mamá* said. He just smiled, a sad smile.

"Papi, *mamá* made your favorite…fried chicken," I said.

"Bueno," he said in a raspy voice.

"I don't know if he could eat that right now. His esophagus is still healing," Mami said.

"It's ok," he said.

"Where is Jairo?"

"In the streets, *mami*, where else?"

"That kid, *coño*! I told him his father was coming today."

"You shouldn't be surprised."

We all sat down at the dinner table and *mamá* began to say a prayer. She always liked to bless the food, she was old school like that.

"*Dios*, thank you for giving us life and for giving us this food we are about to eat. May we all live healthily and happy."

My father had his head down with his eyes open. He had an ashamed look in his face. I think I was the only one that noticed. I heard the door open, then slam. Jairo's signature entrance; he sat on a chair without greeting anyone and dug his head into his food. Mami gave him a sinister stare, but held her anger in. The dinner went smoothly until my father tried to take on the fried chicken. He couldn't swallow the rough meat and my mother took him by the arm and led him to the bathroom. Retching sounds echoed throughout the house, and a tortured groan escaped from within him. I lost my appetite.

I slept with my doors locked at night. It kind of scared me that he was in the house. If he tried to kill himself in his delirium, would he try to kill any of us? I stared at the door, waiting on him to pop up at any moment, but he never came. After a while I thought it was stupid. He was in the same room with mami, sleeping with her, and if she wasn't scared, why should I be? He would spend most of his days locked in their room sleeping. On the days that he would come out, I would try and make conversation, but in the end he would just walk away and crawl into his cave.

I tried at least. Jairo didn't even comfort him with his eyes. He would just walk in and out of the house with a look of disgust. I was disgusted myself, but of him. I felt it necessary to at least try and reason with Jairo. I knew how he felt and why he felt that way, but he had to understand father's situation too. It's not like he could control his delusions. I went into Jairo's room one morning and woke him up.

"Yo bro, wake up, wake up. I need to talk to you."

"Yo fuck off, What the hell do you want? Fuck you waking me up for?"

"I need to talk to you about *papi*."

"There ain't shit to say about *papi*."

"Why you have to be such an ass? You forgot he's the one that raised you. I know how you feel. Everything is messed up and crazy, but you have to give him some support. It's not like he is going to be able to go through this alone. We're his children, and we have to act like it. He was a father to us all those years and now we are going to turn our backs on him?"

"Stop being a bitch. You act like if he was always the best father in the world."

"How can you say that? Don't you remember when he taught us how to play Super Mario Bros. on the Nintendo? We would sit there for hours at a time trying to beat the levels, fighting over who went next, and every time we would get stuck on a world he would show us how to beat it. Or when we got to Bowser, he would take over and say, I'll show you guys how it's done, and then he would kick his ass. Or how about when he used to bring those dried shrimp from Chinatown. We would go through the day just waiting for him to arrive with the shrimp because they were so tasty, and when he would get home with the shrimp we would play and eat shrimp until we got tired. You think all that doesn't count?"

Jairo closed his eyes. It seemed as if he was contemplating what I had said.

"So go help him! What do you need me for?"

"I can't do it alone…"

"Your problem, not mine."

This pissed me off. I was trying to make things better, and he was just brushing every word I say off like dandruff on a black suit. I went over to the foot of the bed, grabbed him by his ankles, and pulled him out the bed.

"I'm going to kick your ass," he said as he stood up.

He pushed me against the wall, and the loud bang of bone hitting the wall resonated throughout the apartment. He was about to punch me in the face when my father stood in front of doorway, staring at us with watery eyes. Had he heard our conversation? My mom ran into the room.

"What in the world is happening over here? Are you trying to bring this damned building down!?"

"Your daughter woke me up, that's what happened."

"Fuck you!" I said

"Jairo, *Cállate coño!* Junior, go to your room, and you,

I'm tired of your shit. You better fix your attitude if you don't want me to fix it for you." Jairo scoffed and laughed.

My mother lost it. She grabbed the closest thing she found, which was an iron, and flung it at Jairo. He was able to dodge it in time. My mother went to pounce on Jairo, but I grabbed her and forced her out the room. I never saw my mother react in that way and never wanted to see it again. I took her to her room and saw that my father just sat in the kitchen, looking out the window lost in thought. All the commotion woke *mamá* up, and I explained what had happened. She said she would fix it and went into Jairo's room.

An hour passed, and they finally came out. Grandmother came out first and smiled at me. Jairo came out after, with a pensive and melancholy face.

"Where's *mami*? I want to talk to her."

"She's in her room, but I'm pretty sure she doesn't want to talk to you right now."

"I know… Bro, I'm sorry for everything. Everything has just seemed like a nightmare. I don't know what to believe or how to feel about all this crazy shit."

"Yea, I know how you feel, but we need to stick together. This isn't going to fix itself in one day. Wait here, I'll talk to mami and see if she's ok to talk.

I went in her room and told her Jairo wanted to talk to her.

"Tell him to come in," she said. I knew she wouldn't be able to deny her oldest son.

I went back to the kitchen to see what my father was doing, and I saw him writing on a small paper. He looked at me and quickly stood up. I stepped back, out of reflex more than anything. He gave the paper to me and told me to read it, because he couldn't tell me myself. It read:

I can't tell you this aloud because the house is full of FBI microphones. They are listening to our every conversation and are aware of our every movement. You have to believe me and you have to help me before they take me away. I can hear them speaking through the walls… They are going to kill me! Don't say anything to your mother because she is not going to believe us.

What the hell? What was this? Was I going crazy? No. I looked up at him and his eyes stared at me as if awaiting my reply. My heart started pounding hard against my chest like a prisoner pounding on his cell wall, wanting to escape. I tossed the paper at him.

"*Coño, papi*, this is all bullshit! Why can't you see that?"

"Bu–"

"No buts, there are no microphones and no FBI! Leave me alone!" I said, running past him and out the door. I needed to calm down. I took a walk outside, taking in the cool fall breeze, and watching the dead fall leaves on the ground. The wind was blowing them around like a tornado. I felt like an idiot for running out on him, but I didn't know what to do. Now I know why Jairo always left; all the pressure would go with it when you ran away from it all. Even if it was just for that slight moment.

A Young Man's Reverie

"Let us scratch the bedrock surface of the subconscious mind where the deeply buried memories lie."

I'm self-deprecating, naturally introverted, slow-witted, and have constant melancholy and semi-depression. Drugs, sex and partying helped fill some of the emptiness in me, but thankfully self-help and improvement filled more of it. In spite of that, I still resort back to negative feelings every other day as a checkpoint of where I am in life, where I was and where I'm going. I try not to think too much about the where I'm going part because I just don't know it too well. Well, I get a feeling, and I don't like to think about it because I don't like the idea. Though with each passing day, as the future becomes present and present becomes past, the reality of aging sets in just that much more. I find myself looking further and further back in life. Let us scratch the bedrock surface of the subconscious mind where the deeply buried memories lie. Forcing it out allows it to really challenge who I've become and more honestly, why I've become that way. It probably starts with one of my earliest memories.

"Shitting my pants"

One of the earliest memories I can remember is of me shitting my pants. Yeah, well not pants but diapers. I don't remember what age I was, but it was young enough to be walking in diapers and old enough for the development of core memory. I want to say I was 2 and a half. Talk about a metaphor to carry throughout your childhood. I've been shitting my pants ever since, but not in the literal sense. You know what, I even remember peeing in the potty and seeking my mother for praise. She was my world back then... was.

"Turning a blind eye on bad faith / I have a long dirty laundry list"

I blame my mother for the majority of the outcome of my life. The good, the bad and the ugly. Deep in her heart she is loving, and boy did she love me a lot as her youngest child. For that, I am a good person overall. Not entirely good but generally good. She also had a dark side to her, almost like a Dr.Jekyll / Mr.Hyde kind of thing. I'm definitely not a bad person. Not entirely innocent but not cynical or cold. I owe that to my mother as well. I also owe the majority of my suffering to my mother. My father kind of gets a pass because he hasn't really been in much my life, but not by choice, or at least I like to think so. He made bad decisions and was put away for a long time, which is a good cop out to why I should hate him, but I don't find it in my heart to do so, I just don't. For my mother, I have a long dirty laundry list of reasons to hate her. Despise her. Resent her. It feels so good to put blame on someone else instead of turning a blind eye on bad faith. Does it really help me, though? Some will say *fuck yah*! I say maybe, maybe not or hmm, depends what is more convenient at the time. Especially when the blame goes to the ideally most influential person in my life.

"Fuck the world and forget it all"

Drugs. I would say drugs have been the catalyst for

fucking things up in my life. They put my father in jail, drove my family to poverty, and turned my mother into an addict. I contribute these life experiences to the reason why I'm a hard-core drug user or drinker. Not weed, not even beer. I have experimented with gateway drugs in moderation, but am scared to death of them for what they've done to those around me. They've caused a downgrade in quality of life that never entirely settled in my head. I went from a happy-go-lucky kid living in a lovely 4-bedroom private house in a good middle class neighborhood with all the toys, games and space a kid could ask for to a broke pubescent teen sitting on a urine-stained mattress on the floor with nothing to call his own in the antiquated apartment of his mother's mechanic who supplied her with her average dose of "fuck the world and forget it all". At the time, I was convinced she didn't love me anymore and had given up on me. That's how it felt, and I rationalized feeling the same way about her. Now that I'm older and out of that situation, I see more that it was herself she didn't love and had given up on more than anything else.

"Let go and let God"

My mother battled with a drug addiction for a very long time. Alcoholics Anonymous, though intended for drinking, helped for all habits. Their first step to recovery is admitting you have a problem. She spent some time attending AA meetings for its teachings, even though she didn't drink, but she didn't tell that to others. I think it's where she met her mechanic. She went there sailing to find hope and instead found herself sinking her ship. Meanwhile, waiting for her, I attended the kids' AA classes where the kids of the parents could talk about their feelings. Here I learned a valuable phrase that helped me back then, which was, "Let go and let God," and another one that would help me a lot later on in life which was the Serenity Prayer. The other kids didn't really take it seriously and used the class more of an advantage to play spin- the-bottle and make out with each other - an occurrence I didn't take part in or observe because I didn't know how to kiss and was afraid of being laughed at, but more so because I didn't think the girls were pretty enough to run that risk for. As I would end up doing for much of my childhood, I sat through the moment or sometimes removed myself from the environment. Like my mother taught me to do about personal matters, I would never speak about it because speaking about things seemed more like self-sabotage. It wasn't hard to hold back because I was already used to not speaking about anything at all. There was a lot of time spent omitting events that could embarrass me or family. As vulnerable as I already was, everything that went on personally had to be confidential. I didn't know how it could come back to affect me. There was only one being that could hear me and not judge me, so I prayed to God a lot back then.

"Mean street wolves who I thought I could call friends"

It was harder in 2002 to distract myself as an early teen. It wasn't like today, when we have smart phones, tablets, and Wi-Fi. Computers with dial-up were expensive as fuck. So I took long walks. Just my thoughts and me. Who else could I reveal my sadness to? Where could I stunt the madness developing in me for not having enough outlets? I sought solitude in similar kids who were out roaming the streets like me. I was a mild, modern-day Red Riding Hood running into mean street wolves I thought I could call friends.

"Sailing down the river"

Each kid had a story of their own. A story about achievement and failure, acceptance and rejection. If you click and vibe with someone, you gravitate towards them, and when you're in desperate need of feeling loved and accepted, your friend recruiting standards drop drastically. The wolf pack bunch I called friends were lost boys - even more than I was. We all had the potential to be better than ourselves, but we didn't know how to. We were drifting with the wind, dancing to the beat of our own drums, and sailing down the river. Unlike the kids I associated with, I wasn't always this way. I wasn't as careless of what lay ahead in my future. I tried hard not to care and even pretended I didn't for a long time, but at the end of each day I faced the truth that I wasn't relatable. I developed the delusional sense of getting back to my old childhood lifestyle and the things I was missing out on as a middle-class kid. More importantly, I just had to get out.

"All we have is each other!"

I got out of that damn apartment but stayed in the same neighborhood. My mother and I shared a basement. Just us two. For a while, It was a pretty tolerable lifestyle for both of us because she let me be, and I let her be. Occasionally, some of my things would go missing. I remember missing a

Nintendo DS, which I later realized she traded in for drugs because I ran into the dealer's son playing with it in the park. Really?! Yeah really, but this wasn't surprising anymore - this was expected behavior from her. I'd look at the bright side; she was the one who paid the rent and helped me find part-time gigs to make a little money for myself, and she would let me stay out in the streets late.

At the same time, she also sometimes asked me step out of the basement late at night to allow an unfamiliar person in to do who knows what for what knows what. I'd rather not know, but I'm sure it wasn't anything admirable. I remember once not having anywhere to go. So I simply sat in a 24-hour Laundromat at 1 am. Watched the hands on the clock turn till I was allowed back in. I sometimes would find where she had her pipe hidden. I eventually grew tired of tolerating her. I came home once smelling the toxic odor of a burnt rock. I rushed to her room and I gave her a piece of my mind. She was in an airbed on the floor. She was sunken into it because much of the air was deflated, and she was too high to care. She was covered in a heavy comforter with a camel and navy-colored royal design looking pattern. I couldn't tell if she was there or not, but I knew she was. I couldn't even tell if she was dead or alive - I really wasn't certain. The room was dark even though it was the middle of the day. There were two or three plastic cups on the floor half-filled with her piss, partially because she had a bladder issue and partially because again she was too high to care. I yelled, "Is this what you've become? Is this what you are? You're rotten. How could you be like this? Don't you see what it's done to you? Don't you see what it does to me? I need you. You're going to kill yourself and I need you. All we have is each other!" I left the house. I vowed, no matter what, I would never be so inconsiderate about the people in my life.

"The system of life checkpoints and balances / Prisoner of my own mind"

Ever since, I came to that realization I've developed a strong work ethic. The harder I work, the more the more I can be helpful, but instead I came to notice the less others do. The less others do, the further ahead I get over them. The further I get, the lonelier it is, and the heavier the burden feels. Similar to the loneliness and burden I felt on that urine-stained mattress while staring at four shadowy walls in an unfurnished room. This is where the system of life's checkpoints and balances starts to arise for me. It reminds me of where I've been and where I want to go. It tells me when to do less and when to do more. It tells me who I think I am and who I think I should be. It's made me a prisoner of my own mind.

Time... Flown and Forgotten

I remember this from when I was sixteen, the very first time I remember noticing something was wrong. My sister had recently immigrated to Canada. When passing by her old apartment made me think of her and I mentioned it to my dad, he seemed lost and had forgotten where she had lived for several years. Progressively, he forgot things here and there. We took him to the neurologist, who diagnosed my dad with Alzheimer's. Being a naïve teenager and having no understanding of the illness at the time, I remember my siblings trying to make sense of the diagnosis, in complete disbelief of how a neurologist diagnosed a 58 year-old with Alzheimer's with no family history and such an early onset. Looking back, I see it all, how it has progressively gotten worse. I now see him slowly fading away.

I moved to the US when I was 19 to study psychology. When people used to ask me what drew me to the field, I would talk about how I grew up wanting to understand people and behavior, and I would mention my dad, that I wanted to help him. Little did I know there isn't much I can do but just understand what is happening to him and watch his suffering. I cannot change what is to come.

I spoke to several of my colleagues about it. From all the bits of advice I got, I remember a few religiously. One, his decision-making power is gone; so we do not give him family decisions to make. And two, Alzheimer's is tougher on the family than on the person who is ill. They exist in their own limited world, and it is the family that sees them suffering. The latter made me cry; I could see myself losing him and him not caring what is happening.

I cannot recall the last time he gave me the correct

day or even the year. He keeps reliving the same difficult moments from his life every morning at breakfast. He keeps on bringing up past bad experiences with relatives even though he made peace with them a long time ago. On his brother's funeral, he forgot that he had died.

Getting him out of the house is a challenge; he becomes aggressive and agitated, and starts swearing on his mother's grave. He hates meeting people, he hates change, and he hates anything outside of his routine. He refuses to consider himself dependent. He refuses to believe that he forgets his way home. He refuses to let my mom do anything on her own or go out of the house. He runs through traffic, not caring if the lights are on Walk. It has become tougher and tougher to make him realize he can't do everything he was capable of doing a long time ago.

My mom has become his crutch, to whom he has become mean and has emotionally disturbed because of the illness. She has gone into self-loathing mode, where she has started to believe that she is what is wrong with this world and that she can never do anything right. She has lost her own sense of self. She is now married to his illness.

The part of my family that lives in Pakistan still fails to understand what he has become. They don't understand the magnitude of the problem. My family in the US, however, has already started preparing the children for what is happening and what will happen.

I just dread the day he forgets me, his beloved daughter he used to call his princess. Reluctantly, one day… I will be forgotten.

The Origin of My Madness

Throughout a child's life, we require very specific formulas for optimum growth. It might be support, acknowledgement, verbal reassurance, a hug, or-most of all-love. These are crucial foundations to a healthy mind that are applicable to children and adults alike. One that is devoid of such feelings is devoid of all warmth life has to offer. We grow up with the preconceived notion that life is a cruel and dangerous place, where there is no protection from the travesty of our manmade society. So it begins, my tale of how I've endured and survived the residual effects of my neglect and abuse.

During my youth, the brief moment of warmth I've felt, as brief as it was laid upon me, the cold grip of reality sets in. My mother, suffering from postpartum depression, unable to deal with the onset of hormones withdrawing from childbirth, laid her misery onto her first-born child. His name was John, and he was a normal boy. As any normal child would, we aim to please our caretakers, as they are gods in our eyes. As "God" would have it, she did as she pleased, unable to control her actions due to her mental affliction. Being that I was a child, I had no choice but to endure it as long as I could.

The types of abuse I've endured were meticulous beatings, where actions were calculated; for example, I'd have to kneel on an abacus, and if I were to slouch, there'd be repercussions for my inability to endure this corporal punishment. There'd be times where I'd be locked in a bathroom in the dark and forbidden to drink water even though I was dehydrated from weeping for long periods of time. Though the physical punishments were cruel, it was the mental damage that was devastating. As my father and grandmother watched helplessly, I would have to endure this for nearly three decades.

With no one to turn to, this started to change the way I saw things. My own mental disorders were developing, and this flowed into my reality. I remember being a peculiar child. Little did I know, this was because my mind was changing. I started to view life for what it was, a cold and hostile place where no one could save me, nor did they care to. Just a damaged child, wandering aimlessly in search for answers and no one would bother, because, why would they? I wasn't their responsibility. My peers didn't understand why I spoke of such harsh subjects, and my teachers thought that I was just a troubled boy. They too, ridiculed me for my misfortune; this made me bitter, and in silence, I grieved for the loss of my innocence.

There were many years spent attempting to connect with others, through grade school into junior high, to no avail. I was unable to find anyone. I remember hearing chatter that the kids thought I was too pessimistic, that I was no fun to be around; they never understood that I was just trying to save myself from the madness that was conjured in my mind. Eventually they resorted to bullying me, because children don't know better. I was the odd one, and because of that, I had nowhere to run once more. I had no peace of mind - I would go home and receive further abuse, and I would go outside and receive the same.

Eventually, I gave up. My grades plummeted because I couldn't focus anymore. I wasn't able to bear the world, as there was not a single day where I would not feel pain.

Upon finishing junior high, I retracted from the world by disassociating myself and locking myself in the same house where the origins of my madness had started. Ironically, my parents wondered why I was falling apart. They couldn't understand it as they were not educated on the subject of child development and mental disorders. They've attempted to correct their mistakes or at least analyze why I became the way I did.

Their first attempt was by putting me in a karate class, hoping this would teach me discipline and provide me with the confidence to progress in life. However, little did they know, my karate teacher had quite an anger problem. There was a time I refused to go to class, and this angered the man. He put a smile on his face for my father, but once he left, he threw me into the dojo where we practiced. Being a small child, it wasn't difficult to ragdoll me around. I recall being punched repeatedly in the face. The room was lined with mirrors. He picked me up with one hand by the neck and pushed me against the glass. He then proceeded to punch me. Eventually, when it ended, I was forced to proceed with my class with all the children looking at my swollen face, tears cascading down my face and sorrow filling my soul. Helpless. Once again.

Anger and rage developed. As people, we are programmed to self-preserve. Anger is a mask for sadness but it is something also used to repel intruders. I was fortunate to be appointed a social worker before I completely stopped going to school. Her name was Ruthine, and she is one of the few positive influences in my life. She made attempts to break through my psyche, but being that my mind was put into self-preservation mode, I was too far gone to be helped, and I needed to discover my own salvation.

Eventually I would run away from home around the age of fourteen. This was my attempt to discover myself and stray away from the painful reminders of my past. This ordeal lasted roughly close to a year. I spent my time residing in different houses of individuals that were equally troubled. If I weren't sleeping at random people's houses, I'd seek shelter inside 24-hour cafes. I ate when there was an opportunity to, usually from the houses that I was fortunate enough to bunk in for the night. As fortunate as I may be, there were dangers to being that young and wandering.

People would take advantage of me in attempt to have me sell drugs, or simply commit acts of crime. I was fortunate in that I knew the difference between right and wrong. Although I would never harm others, I would do things to harm myself. My anger caused me to hit objects, and I feel the damage now that I'm older. Eventually, I would return home, as being homeless was not practical and the individuals I met had played a ruse on me. Friends I thought I made were only people who wanted to use me for their own benefits. As any child, we are easily influenced, and with experience, we learn who our allies are.

From then on, I locked myself in my home for many years. I had stopped going to school, I stopped talking to people in person, and I only went out when I needed to acquire certain things. My parents bought me a computer in attempt to break my trance; little did they know, this strengthened my disassociation. I would spend countless months just looking for things to occupy my time obsessively.

My computer had become a remedy to my lack of a social life. I would have the confidence to speak to others behind a screen, but I would forget what it meant to socialize in person.

I eventually met my first girlfriend - we'll call her Briana. She had taught me something about myself, that I sought love in other females to fill the void that my mother left. I failed, as I did not know how to properly react or treat women. I ended up becoming obsessive. I was insecure about who my partner associated herself with, as I felt inadequate. I would be controlling, I became angry and manipulative, I needed to know every aspect of her life, and I needed to know what she was doing at all times. She eventually left me, as I made her feel like a caged bird. This was not her fault- that much is clear - this was the outcome of a boy who lacked a mother's love and was met with her scorn. All my relationships would fail from that point on, until I would teach myself the concept of self-love.

After many years of wandering aimlessly without a purpose, I eventually went to Elmcor to obtain my GED. Without initial schooling, this was a difficult task as I was plagued with social anxiety and lack of overall confidence in my ability to complete the tasks appointed before me. Sure enough, I completed it, but just barely. At that time, I smoked a lot of marijuana, as it was a coping mechanism for me. During that time, I had no idea that marijuana would be a form of maladaptation. There would be times where it would help, but for the most part, it conjured severe anxiety and paranoia along with ever-expanding thoughts that raced with time.

Upon obtaining my diploma, I went to Job Corps to get my security license. Everything was finally looking up for me. At that point, I even met the love of my life, but sure enough, my past would catch up to me and haunt me. This was due to the fact that I had no knowledge of what my mind was dealing with. I eventually learned that I have PTSD. It's a misconception that only soldiers are able to contract this mental disease. This would apply for any Individual that goes through continued trauma that is left untreated.

Life seemed good at the moment; it was a blissful year for my ex and me before everything fell apart. I had history repeat itself before my very eyes. I had made mistakes I made many years ago, mistreating my ex once more and failing to realize that love is free and not something to be conditioned or controlled. I hadn't understood why I reacted this way, but I've learned that I have abandonment issues. The thing about PTSD is, it can be triggered in unlimited ways. We could be triggered into a flashback by being reminded of something in the past - for me it was her ability to walk away from me. This put me into fight-or-flight mode because I felt abandoned and I became defensive because of it. This was a reminder of my mother, constantly walking away from me when I would cry during my youth, and because of that, I developed this complex around women.

Four years passed. Within that time I was arrested and kicked out of my house. The charges were dropped, and I had once again become homeless. Although I was twenty three at the time and much older, it felt more difficult as the manifestation of my affliction had become stronger than ever. Sorrow drowned all that I knew, and anger had driven me to the brink of madness. My relationship was falling apart, my family couldn't help me, and my friends had abandoned me. I had nothing once more. So I attempted to kill myself.

It was especially cold that day, and what had driven me to decide on such a thing was my ex leaving me. I had decided at that moment that life was not worth living anymore. So I took off my jacket and shirt. I had only my jeans and tank top on at that moment. I knew that if I left my upper half exposed, I could potentially die from pneumonia. I lingered through the cold as my body convulsed in an attempt to warm itself and preserve my vital organs. I did not care anymore; I was ready to die.

Sure enough, the divines clearly had other plans for me. My ex called the cops and the ambulance to restrain me so they could take me to the hospital. My fingers burned as I felt my body sacrificing my limbs to preserve the life that resided within me. Upon my release, I decided to go see a therapist. I needed to make an attempt to retake control of my life and not be smothered by my past. I've taken steps to reform myself, to become a functional adult in our society.

The problem that comes with surviving is that the child that resides within never had the chance to grow. This, of course, comes with complications. For example, our society has a negative stigma associated to those who don't meet certain criteria: not being able to accomplish certain goals "on time", such as school, being married within a certain age, or having enough job experience. With enough things working against us, society doesn't take kindly to those who have walked a difficult path.

As a survivor, we have a duty to our society, to educate others and accept all with open arms--to not make another individual feel alienated, to provide hope and opportunity to others who may not see the love that resides within us. In all of us lies a child that is reaching out to others for love and security. We all reside on this earth together, and we have an obligation to each other to progress as a unity. No one man is able to accomplish everything on his own. Through this same unity, we can spread the message that we are not alone, that there are millions upon millions plagued and suffering in silence. But in silence we shall suffer no more. As you can climb from the depths of your own madness, I personally can't carry you from your own mind, but I certainly can guide you, provide knowledge from my own crucible in the hope that you may learn from my mistakes. From one survivor to another,life can be beautiful;you were made to be this resilient because you have a purpose, you have a place, you can feel love, and you can live the life you dreamt of. We may not be able to rid the world of all wicked things, but we can train each other to be strong enough to handle it. Together, we will create a beautiful world, from one survivor, to another.

About the Author

Furwa immigrated to the US when she was thirteen. Though the love of her culture runs deep she has spent the last couple of years shaping her identity as an American Muslim woman and exploring how the two cultures can compliment each other. Furwa spent the last three years working with  teenagers from all cultures in the Bronx. As she helps them navigate the tumultuous teenage years, she has learned from them kindness, resilience and patience. Her experiences and wisdom have also enriched their world: "Ms. J you have inspired me to be stronger and stand up for myself!" a female student quotes.

Furwa doesn't know what her future path may hold but she hopes to continue find ways to share her love of her culture and guide people in peace and acceptance.

www.ingramcontent.com/pod-product-compliance
Lightning Source LLC
Chambersburg PA
CBHW050420290526
45786CB00003B/1336